Swahili Chronicles

Mark Walker

CONTENTS

I feel very at home when I am travelling through East Africa, nothing seems too much of a problem even though I am a Caucasian.

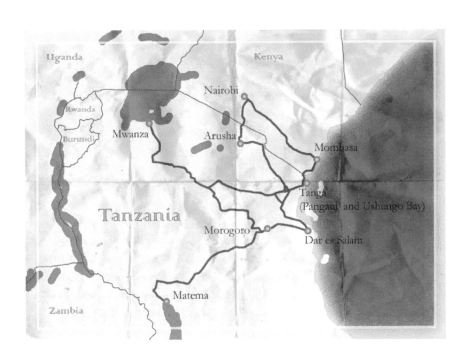

Swahili Chronicles — a journey to the heart of Tanzania

I have been travelling to Tanzania frequently over a period of fifteen years. Usually for no more than one month at a time.

This last journey was different — I chose to disappear and do my own thing for three months. You may well ask, "Why?"

So many people have questions about Africa, yet have never been there.

"Isn't it dangerous?"

"Won't you get ill?"

"Isn't everyone out to cheat you?"

"They're all starving, aren't they?"

Or they give you platitudes.

"Oh, you're so brave!"

"I couldn't do what you do!"

You shall find my response in this collection of short stories, poetry and photographs.

Going Home

The red faced, white skinned man
Is going home
Not to cold, grey skies
Or to granite clad tenement buildings

The homecoming can be felt
Anticipated in every bone and sinew
Sweet and pungent music to my ears

Freedom comes with a hard price tag
A searching, longing
To piece life's jigsaw together

Now a new colour is apparent and alive

Vibrant at times, muted at others

Seen in God's nature
His people and landscapes
That are new yet familiar

Gone are the dark clouds
Of fear and foreboding
Changed to the sunrise and distant horizons

Reachable now as life is content

Years are advancing
Yet youthfulness lingers
As long as I've passion
To live to the full

Follow no leader
React to your conscience
Stirred up emotions
To contemplate later

Love every moment
As if it's the last one
Eager to harness
All that's ahead

So I rest in the knowledge
That money is useless
Seldom buys freedom
Quickly shall tarnish

The red faced, white skinned man
Is going home
Not to cold, grey skies
Or to granite clad tenement buildings

The red faced, white skinned, black man
Has found life in its fullness
In Tanzania

Village reflections

The journey starts in Pangani, a small village on the Swahili coast of Tanzania.

These are my thoughts.

It is early evening, just before sundown, and the cool sea air envelopes the street, save for a few homes lucky enough to have generators or main power.

Yet, as I walk back from the beach and I listen to the waves crashing on the shore, my friends and I also hear the delightful laughter and childhood happiness of kids playing in the street.

"*Mzungu, mzungu*," they cry… or perhaps, "*Shikamoo*," the Swahili greeting of respect to the elders.

One small boy plays in the gutter right next to the red earth road and the shop selling essentials of the day.

All this is done in the shadow of a small solar lamp outside an old ramshackle house.

But I ask you, is this POVERTY?

I don't think so.

I think it is part of a rich childhood.

Boda boda men

We sit in the twilight under a huge, flowering, green tree which gives shade and shelter from the fading sun that is still fierce at this early evening hour.

I am the only *mzungo* amongst seven or eight East African friends, debating the day and the local football match, a 1–1 draw, a conclusion that satisfied the very lively and friendly crowd that had gathered at the *kumba* just an hour or so earlier. The football field lies adjacent to the fast flowing Pangani River. Opposite is a yard used for the shucking of coconuts. Workers are paid on a per piece basis. Lithe fit men and youths slave all day long in the searing heat, torsos bronzed and glistening with toil and sweat, just to earn enough to feed their families for the day.

The sun is now setting over the bus-stand square, which is surrounded by small stalls. The Big Apple Café is close to where we are gathered.

The smell of charcoal flamed meat and frying chipped potatoes is too good to be ignored.

Rashid goes to place our order as we continue to chat.

Suddenly there is business all around as the evening bus arrives from Tanga town, 40 kilometers north on the red earth road.

The *boda boda* drivers rev their motorcycle engines and, with great haste, rush past us to stop beside the bus, hoping for a good fare, as not getting one can mean the difference of having food or no food on the table in the morning.

Karibu sana (welcome again)

Swahili hospitality — *ugali* and goat meat
I usually think a great sign of acceptance from one culture to another is when you are casually asked to dine with people.

I have just finished dinner with Rashid Idrisa and walk back in the dark past people cooking outside over charcoal fires. Kids shout, "*Mzungo*" or "Good evening" as we pass.

Most homes are square, one storey and solidly built with a small, outside, five-foot way where families lounge on mats and rest.

By eight in the evening the temperature has cooled a bit and there is a refreshing breeze from the Indian Ocean.

We turn into the market area where the small businesses are beginning to pack up for the night, though a few stalls still have lights on — perhaps hoping to sell the last of their fresh produce.

Rashid and I say goodnight, thanking each other for yet another great day.

I walk into the Mboni Lodge courtyard to be greeted by Charles and Miriam, the owners, who invite me to eat again.

This time it is *ugali* and goat meat. I don't normally like *ugali*, though this is the best I have ever tasted, and the meat is succulent, having been marinated in salt and lime juice — a perfect ending to the day.

Chai and donuts — a Wednesday morning in Pangani

The morning is lazy, just like the stupefying heat of the sun.

Not a day for walking further than the village market square, I sit with the *boda boda* drivers and chew the fat.

We talk about Malaysia and Tanzania, how hot it is in both countries at this time of the year. Rains had been expected in January, but just a few showery days have arrived — not enough to make anything lush and green. The cattle farmers are having to seek pasture further and further away as all around becomes parched, scorched and tinderbox dry.

I am ready for some tea, so head over to the Big Apple Café — they have good fans — so I can cool down a bit.

I sip hot sweet tea — *chai* as it is known here — and dunk a fresh donut into it. Sublime comfort food.

Rashid Idrisa has a late breakfast of *chapatti* and liver in a tomato-based soup.

We watch the big bus, luggage inside and strapped to the roof, filling up to go to Tanga.

Sometimes the road is so rutted that the bus crawls from side to side like some demented mechanical crab, trying to get a foothold and some grip to continue the torturous journey.

The burning of boats in Ushongo Bay

Ushongo Bay, situated right on the Indian Ocean, is a village unaffected by the ravages of time and so-called progress. The fishermen still use traditional methods untouched for centuries.

I am taking an early evening walk past the youths playing a hard game of football while the mothers, kids, and elders sit further up from the sand near their homes made of palm thatch and wood. In the middle distance, I spot a fire under the hull of a boat. At first I am concerned that no one is gathering water to put it out!

I then see more petrol being put carefully around the triple-hulled small-sailed outrigger, or *ngalawa*, as it is called in Swahili. I ask, "What is happening?"

"Ah, we are not burning the boats. We are putting tar on the hull to waterproof it!"

Another cultural lesson learnt.

In Harmony

I am in perfect harmony
Body, soul and spirit
I will often think
Of this time to come

When troubled by the day's thoughts
The harshness of reality
Yet, here I sit in perfect harmony
A friend, across from me

In silence, yet deeply connected
I had never left this place
Carrying it like an amulet of peace
Always there, to lean on

For security, succour, warmth
Away from the raw horrors that invade each day
On television screens or print
My mind is still and calmed by friendship that's serene
In Tanga town, am all at ease.

The amazing Mr. Clinton

"So, my dear Mark," is always the solicitous way in which he starts
the conversation, as I sit with Rashid Idrisa and his good friend
Pancho under the umbrella of the Tigo phone stall. It all happens so
innocently by me saying, "Hi," and starting polite conversation with
one of the characters that surround the bus stand stalls in sleepy
Pangani. Clinton Fumigation company and Mr-so-my-dear have their
eyes on the prey — and that is me. "Come view my small shop, my
business has great potential for a foreign investor like you, my dear."
As he continues to show me worming tablets for cattle and rat
poison, I am sure he has the wrong man under his spotlight. Clinton
had been a UN army man in his time, a fit man for all of his seventy
years, but he likes a drink or two — and a woman or three — to
spend his time and possibly the investor's cash on. This is one golden
opportunity I am not handshaking on.

"I am not friends with chillies," salty rubber tyres or a stomach full of octopus

Late afternoon tales from Tanga
I had an early breakfast while looking out over the gardens towards the sea. Early because I am on a mission — a great and wonderful accomplishment to attain before leaving this laidback and quiet town. I am making my late morning pilgrimage to the Blue Room Café.

The Blue Room is a must for their meat kebabs and nylon (potato fritters, served with coconut chutney, limes and salted chillies). Rashid and I sit down, look at the food and laugh as I remember our time last year when I asked if he wanted the salted chillies. His quick witted reply was, "the chillies and I are not friends."

This last day together is full of those laughter moments. Rashid decides that by 4 p.m. he is peckish again. We amble over to the food gardens overlooking the sea. I eat a snack and he eats what looks like a whole char-grilled octopus. "Have a try," he says. I do. "Tastes like salty rubber tyres," I say.

Great memories to hold on to.

Salted eggs and oranges
Started the journey today from the hot and dusty streets of my beloved Tanga town. It's a bit like Penang must have been fifty years ago — wide grid-like main streets with narrower connecting side streets, full of heritage buildings in poor repair.

We travel by small coaster bus for the three hours up to the hill town and cooling weather of Lushoto. We stop at Mwheza on the way and are soon besieged by people selling all sorts of foods for the journey — from salted eggs to oranges.

Pass the baby on the left-hand side

Dala dala journeys are always interesting. How people react to being together on a bus fascinates me.

Well let me tell you, the Tanzanians are a very sociable and trusting race. People pass money from the back to the conductor at the front. They put bags on seats to reserve them, and then go to do some shopping before the bus fills up. Their space will not be taken.

Better still is the way the whole community on the bus looks after children. It is a brilliant sign that they do not fear the "bogey man." Mum finds a seat for herself and one boy of about five. She still has a small baby to look after. But that stress is taken from her, as the man on the left causally lifts the child onto his lap and is a surrogate father. Try doing that in the Westernised World, where we now fear our own shadow.

Lost

He sits among the mess of his own awfulness. At first I think I have just passed a pile of debris. Then the pile moves and squirms — it is not only black plastic bags, empty water bottles and remnants of food. There is someone alive but lost.

It is a disturbing sight. This man in tatters, with matted hair and head sores, is awaking, lying in his own filth, yet only two seconds walk from here is one of the main crossroads in Dar es Salaam.

What had happened in his life? Maybe no one will find out. To me the man might be close to the end of his miserable existence.

Was it always this way? He has fallen through the net and down a precipice.

Haunting in Dar es Salaam.

The two sides of Dar es Salaam

Dar es Salaam is a huge sprawling mess of a place. In the late 1950s it had a population of only 128,000. This number has grown, in a mostly haphazard way, to around four million.

Yet I can still feel the history of the earlier years when I am in the downtown Arab Quarter or within the bustle of Kariakoo market, which is one of the largest wet and dry good markets in East Africa. Situated on the Indian Ocean, Dar es Salaam is also one of the busiest ports in the region.

You see, Sir, the problem is...

I have heard this so many times on my travels to Tanzania.

"You see, Sir/Pastor/Teacher/*Mzee*...," or whatever title they choose to bestow on me,

"We have no job, money, transport."

"The machine broke."

"The Government ate the money."

"The donor withdrew, etc., etc."

Very few times did I hear, "Well, Sir, the solution may be...."

It was therefore so refreshing to hear of possible answers to Tanzania's challenges, coming from my friend Philipo.

He is one smart young man, who goes out to ask for work, tells the prospective employers what his skills are and the benefits of employing him to that company.

He has work and does freelance information and communication technology training. If only others would think this way and not expect people to know they need work or have to bribe to get it.

Clinking coffee cups, heated charcoal — a morning walk in Dar es Salaam

Al Uruba Hotel is an ideal place to walk from in the early morning — very close to the main market area of Kariako. I walk, phone in hand, taking photos of local street life.

People here tend to go to sleep early and rise early for work, and the streets are packed with humanity by 7 a.m.

I pass the old-fashioned bicycle knife grinders, homeless waking up on the pavements, women sitting crossed legged on mats selling fruits and the rich aroma of local coffee hitting nostrils at nearly every street corner.

Making coffee is usually carried out by men, who use huge kettles that sit on hot charcoal. Small coffee cups, little more than thimble size, are precariously balanced on top of the kettle. This is all held together in one hand with a triangular bamboo frame. In the other hand is a pail full of small snacks, or "bites" as they are called here, usually finger food such as cake or *samosa*.

On the corners, men huddle around and read the selection of the day's newspapers, laid out on trestle tables, while street sweepers attempt to clear the deep, open flood drains.

Further on, a really jolly Muslim man notices me taking photos. "I am so happy to see you in my city," he says. "Can you please take my photo?"

"*Asante sana rafiki,*" is my reply. Yes, thank you my friend. We have an instant short friendship.

All this and more in downtown Dar es Salaam — feeling wonderful.

Terrace tales — life from rags to riches

I am sitting on the small terrace that overlooks the narrow side street leading down to Kariakoo market. Life in all its ironic absurdity, is there to observe.

It is like a modern take from a Dickensian novel — the street boys lounging in a laconic but menacing manner, with cigarettes dangling from their mouths and a foot against the wall.

People on bikes that are dangerously stacked high with boxes, to be delivered to the market.

Taxi touts bargaining in good humoured nature, housewives laden with shopping, some of it precariously balanced on their heads.

A salesman selling mosquito nets, pure white but easily spoilt if a car passes through the nearby puddles, for it was raining hard last night.

Then a big man in the large new Range Rover pulls up outside the Barclays ATM, swaggering out his rich man's wagon with an air of superiority. Probably here to withdraw more than the average worker's monthly income in one foul swipe of a card.

Life in all its fullness in Kariakoo, Dar es Salaam

Life on the edge

Midday sun is beating down after early morning rains. City centre drains can't cope and the inevitable traffic chaos ensues. I walk up past the lawyers in gowns and collars, taking respite in the nearby café.

Yet, on the edge of a nearby window, lies a young life in tatters. He is literally sleeping at the sharp end. Sixteen or seventeen, perhaps, so much potential wasted, hopes dashed, run into a brick wall.

The pain of life pissed in the gutter.

They are the dark shadows in the sunlight.

A reminder of how unjust and unfair life can be in the big city.

Where for some, the pavement cracks are wide and falling down is inevitable.

A fishy tale for breakfast

It has been raining heavily all night. It woke me up twice, so I decided to sleep a bit later and stroll down to the café around 9.

It is quiet, as this is a day of rest for most people in Tanzania — only essential shops are open, much like in Scotland thirty years ago.

I spot the tall handsome guy speaking to the *chapatti* men at the doorway. He is soaking wet but well dressed, with a quality backpack. He passes all the locals and pulls up a chair at my table.

He greets me with, "*Shikamoo*," the polite way to speak to elders. I understand a little of his Swahili, something about Samaki, Kigoma and a Safari Kubwa.

I tell him that my Swahili is limited, and he then breaks into perfect English. "I sell the big fish from Kigoma. I have come a long way to find a *muzungu* like you. Would you like to become my distributor?"

So, I now add "Fish Salesman" to my long line of possible vocations while here in wonderful Tanzania.

Kilimanjaro Express

The name of the train is misleading, as it goes nowhere near Kili. Instead it meanders its way slowly south from Dar es Salaam to Zambia. Carriages and engines are from the 1970s and probably not changed much since then.

A first class sleeper is adequate and four berth, second class is a soft seat, third is a wooden bench.

The line is a real achievement of Chinese engineering. They see a mountain, and then blast their way through. There are numerous long tunnels and spectacular narrow bridges with huge drops and one or two mangled goods wagons at the bottom — a sharp reminder that things can go wrong.

My companions are a very serious American student from New York, who is going back to work in a lodge on Lake Malawi, and a shoe salesman from Lusaka, who had been in Dar to place big orders from China.

Both are good company.

I arrive in Mbeya and stop at the lovely small guest house called The Peace of Mind, which I have in abundance here in Tanzania.

The poverty of education, the education of poverty

As a seasoned traveller to Tanzania, I thought I understood many of the situations that cause poverty – poor health, malnutrition and other ravages of economics – but I was wrong. It took my good doctor friend, Simon, to explain the effects of the lack of good education and the consequences on health.

I had passed many local village markets, stalls groaning with the weight of fresh vegetables, fruits, poultry, and such. So, why did I see many kids with poor skin, distended stomachs and other obvious ailments?

Seemingly the local villagers believe that the eggs, chickens, fresh vegetables and fruits are only for the rich!

They sell all that is good and nutritious and buy manufactured and processed foods, as for the villagers, such goods are a sign of their sophistication. They can show off to their neighbours that they bought something imported. Meanwhile, their health gets worse.

Doctor Simon and his colleagues are busy in the rural areas trying to change mindsets. They start with the village elders and hope that new and good health education shall be passed on.

The only way out of poverty is education.

The shape of things to come

I am travelling by bus from Mbeya down south to Kyela, a small border town only four kilometers from Malawi.

The road journey is incredibly scenic — following the spine of the hills — with wonderful vistas to left and right. Tea plantations, bananas, pineapples, sunflowers, rice paddies — all there in abundance.

Colours of nature, so bright, it's as if you are taking a part in a 1950s Technicolor movie.

We stop in many villages on the way. At the roadside stalls, there are piles of the freshest produce — tomatoes, cabbages and apples, to name but a few. I look again and notice the apples are not shiny, tomatoes are not all uniform in shape or colour. But I can tell you, they taste wonderful — full of flavour, not full of water.

Give me fresh farm produce anytime and I shall enjoy it 100% more than that sanitised version bought in a big supermarket.

A village banquet

We sit at a village stall. We bought all the veggies for a salad. Emmanuel Elyon Swallow prepares it, as the mama who owns the stall cooks the two kilograms of fried pork and plantain. We wash it all down with soda, while listening to the rain.

The mama is so funny. She says that, although not officially part of our group, she had cooked so would eat with us.

She has this glint in her eye, starts singing a traditional song for me while watching the lightning in the distance.

The girls are sitting next to the pavement in the twilight, braiding each other's hair. People run by with black plastic bags on their heads to save getting too wet.

Pure enjoyment.

The mysterious case of the Castle milk stout — lost in translation in Bukoba

It was good to have some time to myself yesterday afternoon.

I walked down to the lakeshore, enjoyed watching the sea eagles soaring above me — the herons wading in the shallows, then flying off into the distant blue sky. I felt so relaxed and decided to stop at the Bukoba Club for a beer, before returning to the Lake Hotel.

That was where the fun began!

The young barman came over.

"Can I please have a Castle milk stout?"

"Yes, we have it," was his reply.

Five minutes later, he came back — not with a Castle milk stout but a Castle lager, which I find too gassy.

"I am sorry. Do you not have milk stout? You know, the black beer. The Castle milk stout?!"

"Sir must mean the Castle milk stout," was the reply, emphasis on the "ST."

"Yes," I said and laughed to myself.

I drank it with pleasure, in the sunshine, remembering an old British comedy sketch by the Two Ronnies: "Fork handles? We don't have these. Oh you mean four candles?"

The reality of student life

I have many Facebook friends throughout the World and I keep in regular contact with at least two hundred.

One such friend is Sirkubalyenda Kubalyenda who stays very close to Morogoro in a small village called Sangasanga, which means "arrive, arrive."

Well, it took me ten hours to arrive, arrive at Sangasanga from Mbeya. The road was good but very narrow and steep at times, especially near the town of Iringa. Lots of wildlife was seen as we passed through the Makumi National Park: elephant, opaki, giraffe and many small deer.

Reached my friend's place by 6:30 p.m. The welcome was very warm and genuine.

Am staying in his room or student ghetto for two nights. The toilet and bathroom are both outside, and the cooking is done in the courtyard.

His friends, Nelson and Dominic, joined us for a delicious meal of rice, cashew nut stew, green vegetables with avocado, oranges and banana. All are studying Bachelor of Education at the local government university.

Slept at 11 p.m., but am writing this at 6 a.m., as Kubalyenda has been up since 5 a.m. to prepare for a small exam.

Mist, mud and a Mercedes

I hate goodbyes. I prefer to say, "'Til we meet again." My mood yesterday morning was a bit melancholic, as I didn't wish to leave my student friends — for in two short days, they had become like brothers to me.

We arrived at the main bus stand at Morogoro. The mist had settled on the mountains, and the rain tumbled down, making the ground a sea of brown squelchy mud.

The buses coming from Dar es Salaam are all late due to the weather. I have been sitting too long in the car and now need to pee. But OH! the MUD !

Well, a man's got to pee. So I brave the elements and get soaked, sandals stained and wet, caked with a new brown icing.

Then my friends ask me, would I like to travel in a Benz down to Singida, a town eight hours south, on my way to Mwanza? So I end up sharing the ride with the driver and three others, at the same cost as a bus fare. The Merc B200 was a Japanese import being delivered all the way from Dar to Burundi.

Sunshine, showers and surprises — a late afternoon walk in Musoma

Amaziah, Wango and I are spending two days together in the small town of Musoma, which sits on a peninsula close to the Kenyan border in Northwest Tanzania. The townspeople make their living mainly from fishing in Lake Victoria, farming, small local shops and other businesses. It's a sleepy and laid back place.

Around 5 p.m. seems a good time to go for a walk down to the fish market and the ferry pier.

The streets are lined with single-story shops from the colonial era — some with five-foot ways to cover you in the event of rain.

We stroll in the middle of the sandy road towards the lake. The scene reminds me of the old Western cowboy movies when the strangers reach town — minus the Smith and Wesson revolvers.

The dark clouds are mulling over the other side of the lake. But we take that as a great photo opportunity, having sunshine in front and darkness in the background.

Suddenly the wind howls. The storm comes our way. We run as fast as we can into the nearest local café, squashed with over fifty others, rain battering down. Eventually seats are found, new friendships are made with a family from Nairobi, and I receive an invitation to meet them before I fly home. Sunshine, showers and surprises.

Petrified passengers preaching on public transport and other peculiarities of coach travel in Tanzania

Amaziah and I caught the early morning coach to Mwanza, after spending six wonderful days together with Emmy in Bukoba, a small town on the shores of Lake Victoria. Pastor Emmy was on his way back to Kampala.

The journey was ok but uneventful — until we reached a weigh bridge, of which there are many in Tanzania.

We had picked up quite a few passengers who were squashed three into seats for two. Suddenly the coach conductor told us to shut all the curtains and the extra passengers to crouch in the aisle, as the bus went through on the green light.

Seemingly this happens a lot now, as the extra illegal fares supplement meagre incomes.

Everyone was reseated, and then a passenger decided to get up and preach the gospel to everyone. Try doing that on a bus in the UK or Malaysia.

Travelling sometimes brings up more unanswered questions. I constantly have to revalue what is development and if progress is really to the benefit of the local population. Often I doubt that.

Rape of My Homeland

They took my land first
Told me and my village
It was all for the better
An improvement will come
Soon

We are still waiting.
The road's here now
Heavy trucks and all
Go right past our corner
Bypassed

The mine is up the road
You see — gold, I think
Pennies for me
If am lucky

False promise
The white man replaced
By the yellow man
The story repeats itself
Better if they just
Raped us

Yes, it's strong, I know
It's true though
Still have no water
No jobs or security
Bewilderment

At least before this
We had land
Provided, meagrely for family
They took it away
For the road

Body and soul, feel useless
Cheated and violated
Without true consent
It's progress
You know

Crowds, cattle, chickens and cicadas

We had taken the very packed *dala dala* from Magu down about fifteen kilometers to catch the motorbike over to Gran and Grandpa's village.

The bus was so busy that one man exited via the back window into the oncoming traffic. I guess he thought that was easier than trying to squeeze past twenty-two others stuffed like sardines in a can!

Grandma is seventy-seven and Grandpa is eighty-eight, still both fit and well. Rest is not in their vocabulary — it's a hard, hard daily life.

The greeting was so warm, hugs and prayers said for our safe arrival.

Grandpa never sits still, we walked for fifteen to twenty minutes, past his herd of cattle and the small hills made of rounded boulders, unique to this part of Northwest Tanzania.

Later, we spotted him stripped to the waist, cutting and cultivating his plot. He still has the look of a soldier, strong despite his increasing age. He came to the clearing to greet us, it was a very emotional moment, we had last met in 2013, and we pray for each other regularly.

Amaziah and I left grandpa, as he said he had something to do.

So, as evening time descended, we sat outside and chatted. Grandpa came with a live chicken. Now all was becoming clear. This was in honour of me, his guest.

I watched as the chicken was slaughtered, fast and without too much pain. Later we ate, while listening to the cicadas and with the brightest stars shining in a moonlit sky.

Village life in Tanzania.

Leaving Tanzania with a thankful heart

I have been travelling for two and a half months in one of the friendliest countries on Earth.

I am so grateful to the wonderful friends who are like close family to me.

I leave feeling immensely proud to have had the privilege of being accepted into your communities, to have experienced village life, to have enjoyed local food and the hospitality of strangers who have become lifelong friends.

I thank God for all of you — too many to mention individually — you know who you are.

Love and good wishes to all of you. I am not saying goodbye. I am saying, "'Til we meet again."

Notes

boda boda	motorbike for hire with driver
chapatti	unleavened flat bread
dala dala	small overcrowded mini bus
kumba	playing field
Mzee	respectful name for older or wise man
samosa	small spicy Indian snack that is fried or baked
ugali	stiff porridge of maize, millet, or cassava flour

ABOUT THE AUTHOR

Mark Walker is a teller of stories, a poet, writer and photographer. *Swahili Chronicles*, is his first book. To arrange a "Swahili Chronicles" evening of storytelling or a photography shoot, please contact Mark at mark.walker@gardenbenchpublishing.com.

Made in the USA
Monee, IL
11 June 2021

71008586R00036